Clarence H. Carter
Favorite Son

Bathsheba Monk

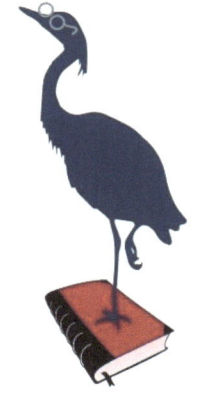

Blue Heron Book Works, LLC
Allentown, Pennsylvania

Copyright © 2018 Bathsheba Monk
All rights reserved.
ISBN-13: 978-1720359876
ISBN-10: 1720359873
All images in the Personal Inventory as well as the cover image are owned by the author and are represented by
Wolfs Gallery, Cleveland, Ohio
http://wolfsgallery.com/

Cover Image:
Clarence H. Carter (1904-2000)
Eggs Rising in Vast Landscape, 1973
pencil on paper laid on cardboard
signed and dated '73 upper right
22 in. h. x 30 in. w.

Blue Heron Book Works, LLC
Allentown, Pennsylvania
www.blueheronbookworks.com

For Blake, Clarence's favorite son

Table of Contents
A PERSONAL INVENTORY 1

POOR MAN'S PULLMAN 17

ABOUT THE AUTHOR 39

A PERSONAL INVENTORY

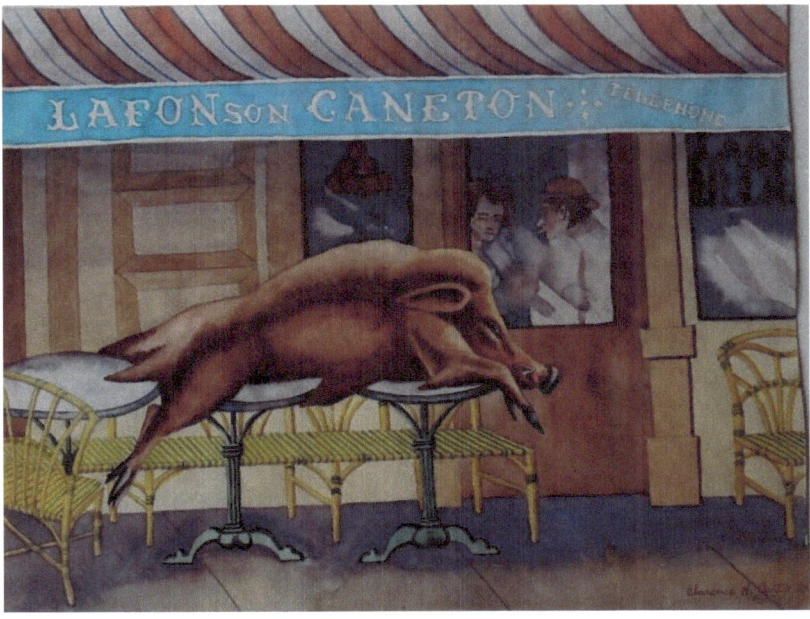

LaFonson's Pride 1928
watercolor on paper
signed and dated '28 lower right inscribed Paris
13 in. h. x 16 1/2 in. w.

Although Clarence is always positioned as a regional American painter, and the heartland is indeed his home, what makes him unique is his ability to absorb other cultures into his work. These influences give his work a spice and sophistication unusual for American Regionalists. LaFonson's Pride was painted in 1928 during one of the many trips Clarence and Mary made to Europe. The owner of this restaurant had just bagged a wild boar and displayed it proudly before butchering it. Blake and I enjoyed this painting in our condos in the Back Bay and then Beacon Hill in Boston.

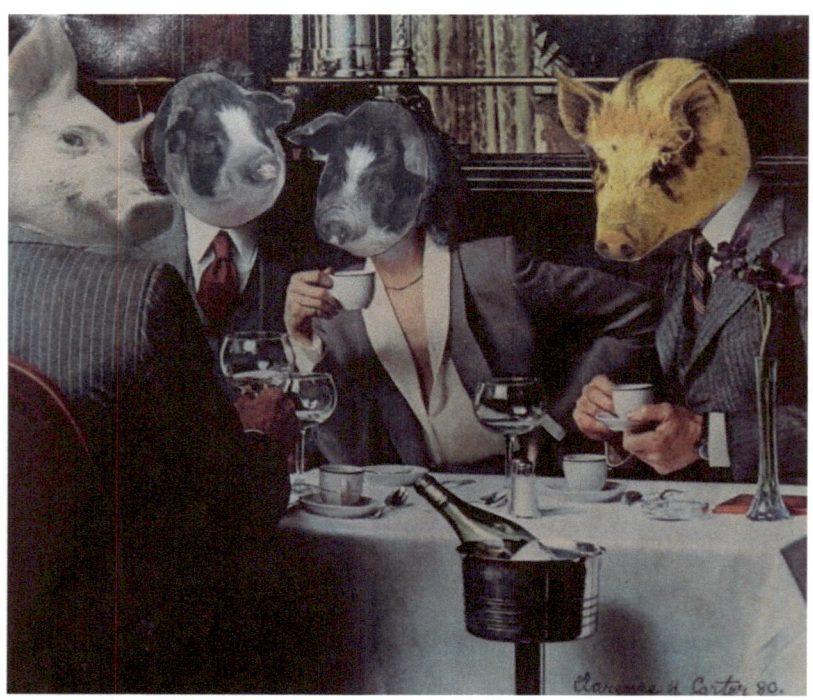

Is that so?
1980
collage
signed and dated '80 lower right
5 ½ in. h. x 6 in. w.

Clarence had a wicked sense of humor on par with his sense of social absurdity. I remember when he did this collage in 1980. Yuppies were just becoming a social phenomenon and Clarence was struck by their self-importance and entitlement.

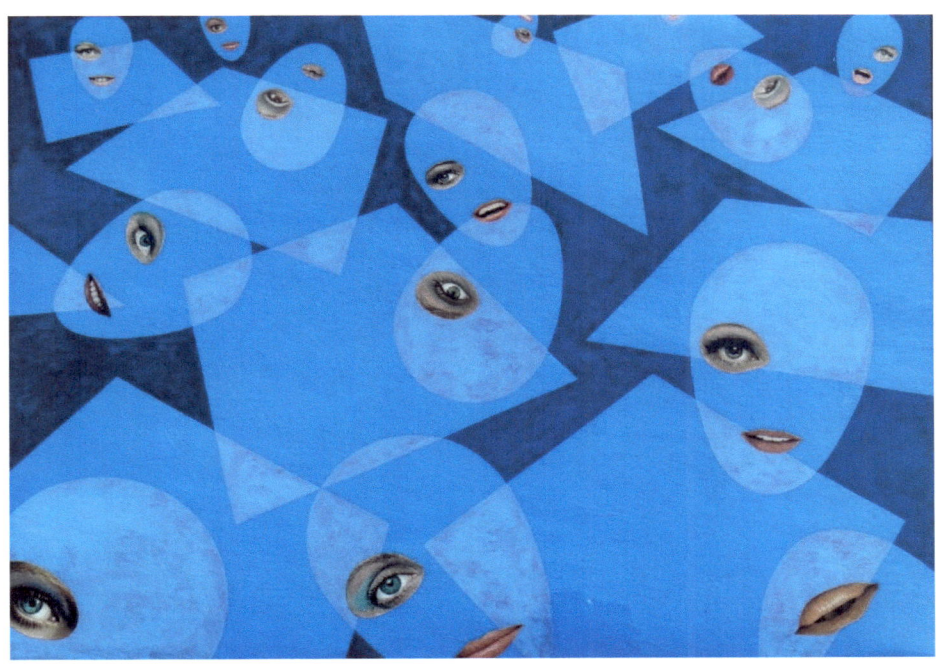

Phantom Ladies, 1979
acrylic and collage on scintilla
signed and dated '79 lower right
30 in. h. x 22 in

This is the quintessential Clarence H. Carter in my opinion. The egg shape of life, the architectural precision, the color exactness. It also reflects Clarence's appreciation of female beauty which he saw centered in the face: the eyes and mouth. Clarence loved women in a way that seems evolved in these times. He appreciated strong women—his mother, his wife of course and his sister Irene. Is it any wonder women loved him? This piece hung in our music room—Blake on tenor saxophone, me on vocals—for years.

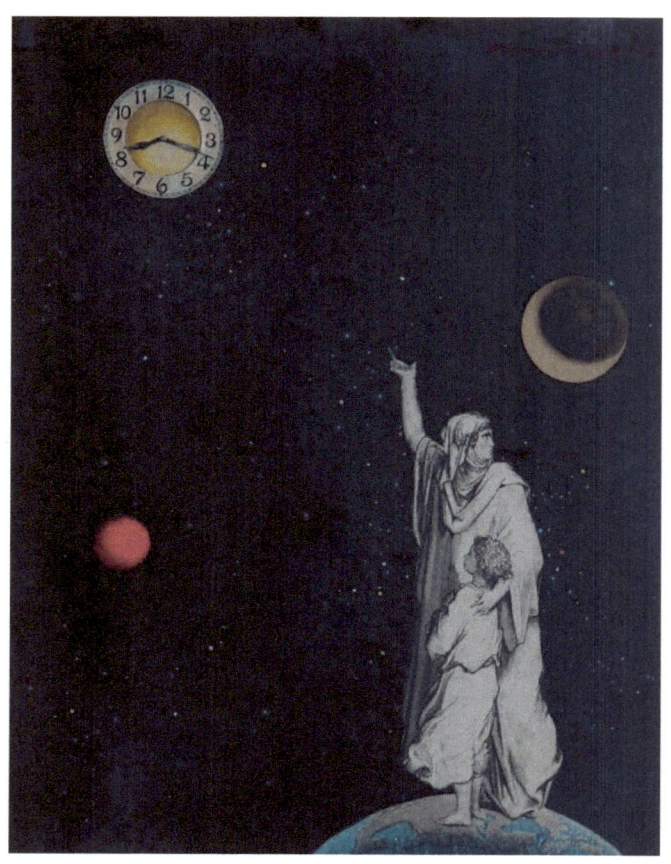

It's Time, 1974
collage
signed and dated '74 upper right
10 1/2 in. h. x 8 1/4 in. w.

This is a very personal piece. It was 1974 and Blake and I had been married the year before. We were home from Europe for Christmas and Clarence hadn't bought a present for Blake. He had intended to buy him a watch, but somehow it wasn't there on Christmas morning. So Clarence went out to the studio early Christmas and made this collage for Blake. I think he liked it better than a watch.

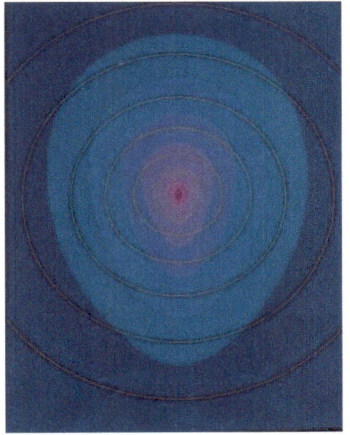 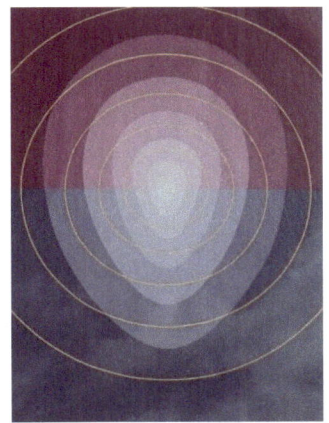

Mandala #5, 1968
acrylic on scintilla
signed on verso
29 1/2 in. x 22 in.

Mandala #4, 1968
acrylic on scintilla
signed '68 lower right and verso
30 in. x 22 in.

Scintilla is a paper that Clarence developed with the Riegelsville paper mill in Riegelsville, New Jersey. Now defunct. Clarence loved to collaborate with other artists and artisans on materials and this is definitely a winner. The paper has an uneven texture that gives depth to otherwise flat media like acrylics. I always loved the colors in these two as well as the golden circles that add a counterweight to the mandalas. They weren't painted as a pair, although I think they complement each other wonderfully.

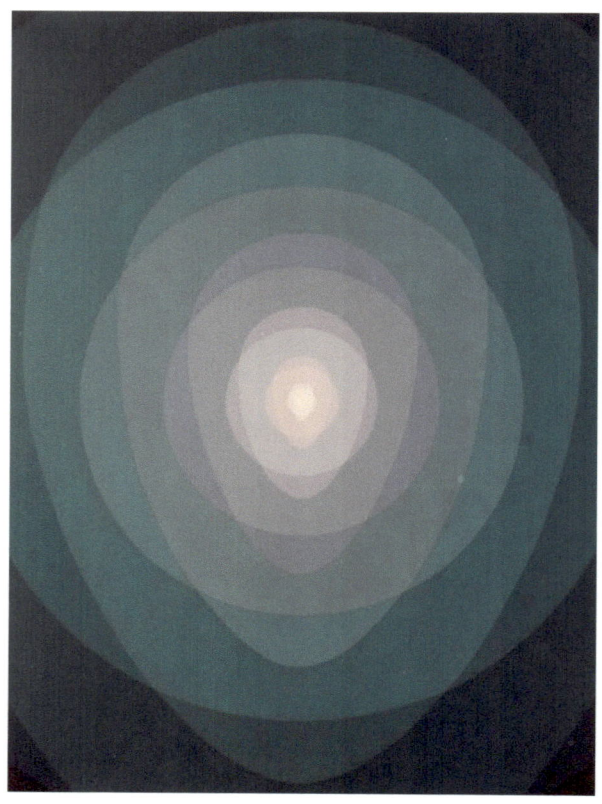

Icon Cruciferon, 1972
acrylic on canvas
signed and dated 1972-73 lower right
50 1/4 in. h. x 36 1/4 in. w.

This is a beauty and presided over many parties at our homes in Europe, Boston, and Pennsylvania. The mandalas are pure Carter and the colors are something you can get lost in for hours. The thing that surprised me about the technique Clarence used to paint these, though, is that he didn't glaze one layer on top of another, as I initially assumed, but he meticulously painted each segment separately, going through his voluminous files of cuttings and color swatches to find the exact color he was looking for. The color files are now in the archives at Southern Ohio Museum. As a personal aside, one autumn I bought a red decorative cabbage and as the winter wore on into a wet spring, the cabbage started to bleed colors—the exact colors in this paining.

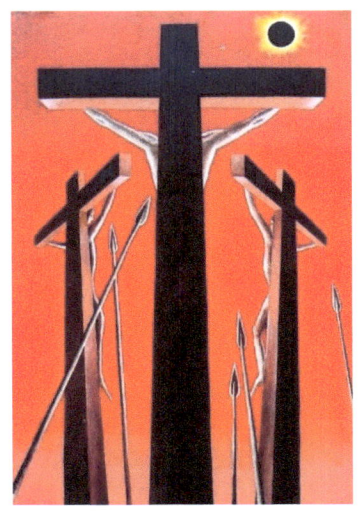 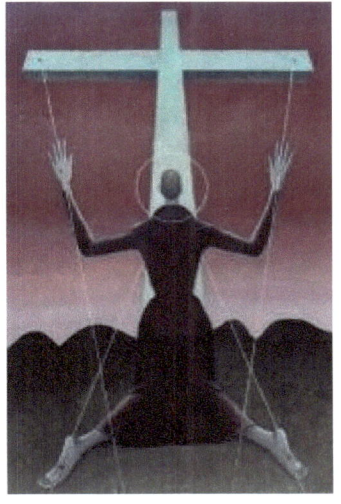

Christ and the Thieves, 1961
acrylic on scintilla
signed and dated
36 in. h. x 24 in. w.

St. Francis before the Cross, 1964
acrylic on scintilla
signed and dated '64 upper left
36 in. h. x 24 in. w.

Clarence and Mary made a lot of trips to Europe and Clarence was definitely influenced by the classicism of European art. In fact, right out of art school, Clarence spent a summer in Capri studying with Hans Hoffman. Although Clarence wasn't influenced by Hoffman's style—Hoffman, according to Clarence, told Clarence to do his own thing and they would discuss Carter's paintings on their own terms later—he couldn't help but take in Hoffman's superb color sense and the proportions of the surrounding architecture and landscape. As an aside, Clarence designed the new steeple of their UCC church in Milford, New Jersey, which I admired long before anyone told me he designed it. These paintings, too, hung in the vestibule of that church for years.

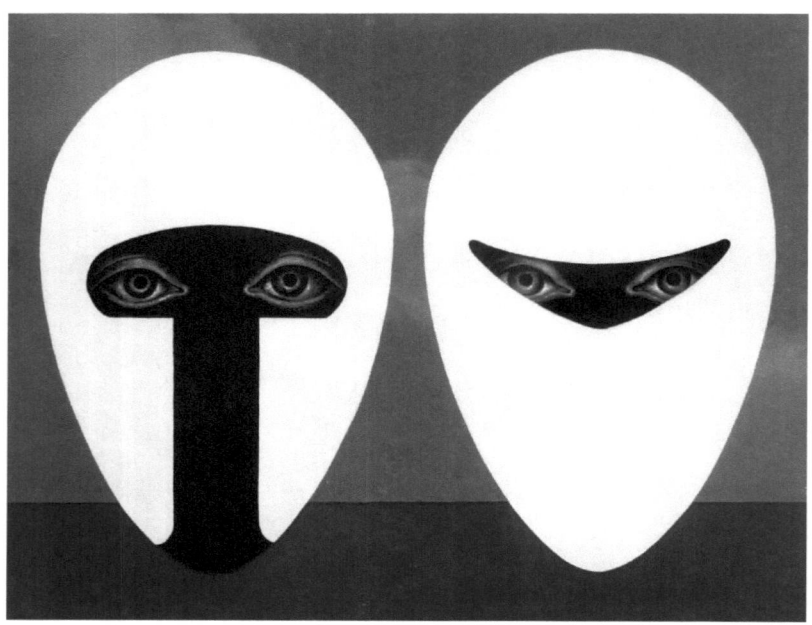

Medieval Heads, 1966
acrylic on scintilla
signed and dated '66 upper right
23 1/2 in. h. x 30 in. w.

These mesmerizing heads looked over me when we were going through a rough patch. I believe there's magic or a healing aura in certain objects and this creation is one of them.

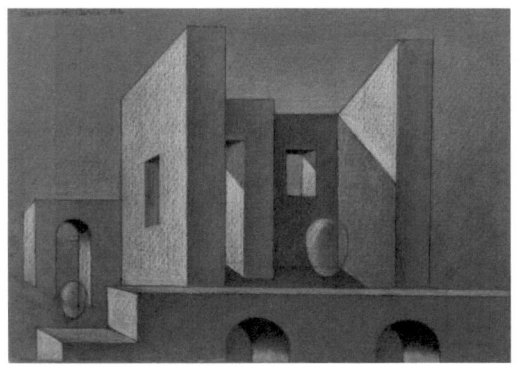

Haunted Memories, Study, 1986
pencil and colored pencil on paper
signed and dated '86 upper left
7 in. h. x 9 in. w.

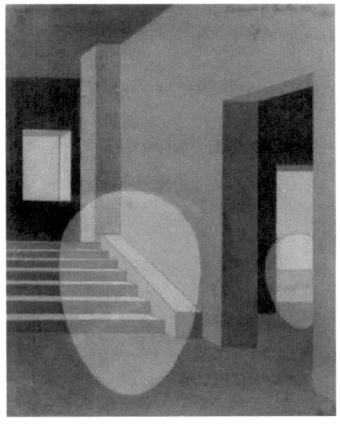

Study for Visitation #1, 1980
pencil and colored pencil on paper
signed and dated '80 upper right
9 3/4 in. h. x 7 3/4 in. w.

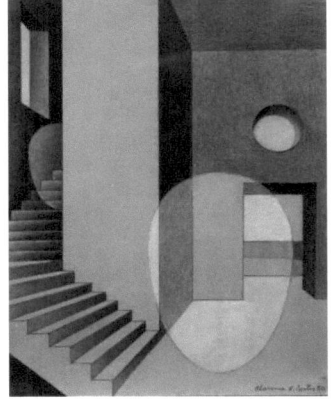

Study for Visitation II, 1980
pencil and white heightening on paper
signed and dated '80 lower right
10 in. h. x 8 in. w.

These seaside architectural drawings (studies for later paintings) are serene and soothing They were the focus of many yoga classes and private meditation sessions I led in my home studio. And yes, they haunt my dreams. Clarence understood and respected our spiritual natures.

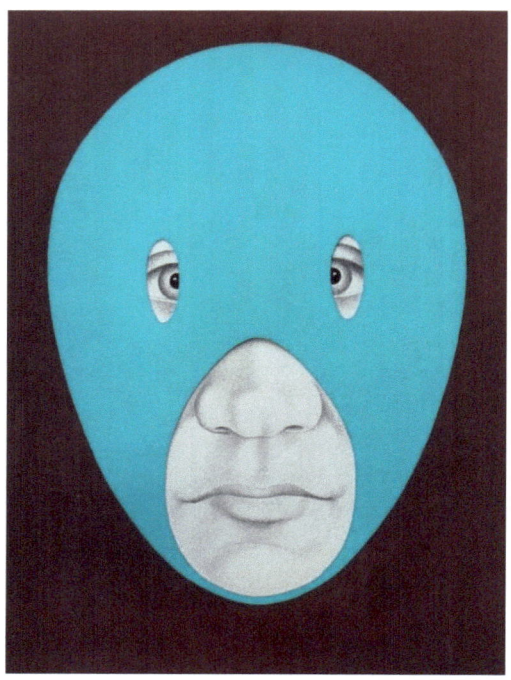

Masked Man Self Portrait, 1970
mixed media collage on scintilla
30 in. h. xl 22 in. w.

Clarence was a very handsome man and so it's funny that he never painted a self-portrait that showed that aspect. He was, as all artists are, the spectator, the observer, the filter through which life pours in and comes out in an exalted form. Nothing captures that essence more than his Masked Man Self Portrait.

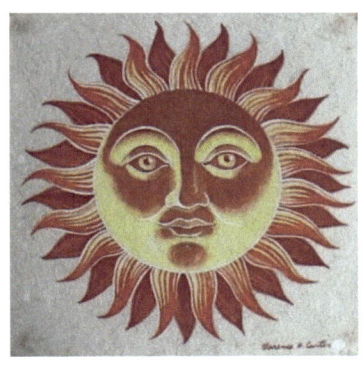 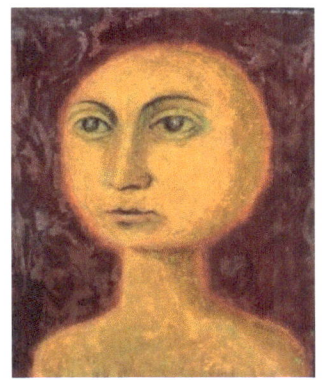

Sun
1960
acrylic on scintilla
signed lower right and verso
11 in. h. x 11 in. w.

Orange head
1961
mixed media on paper
signed upper right '61
25 in. h. x 20 in. w.

It's fun to see Clarence's approach change from flamboyant to minimal during the 1960s. I like them both and hung them together.

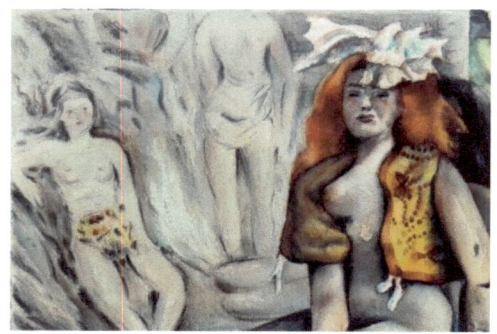

Reveron's Ladies, 1946
watercolor on paper
signed and dated '46 upper left
22 1/4 in. x 15 in. w.

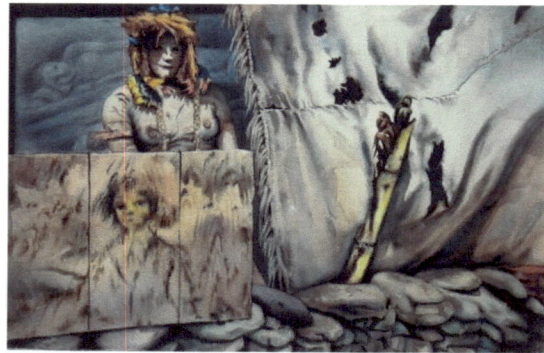

Macuto Mannequin, 1946
watercolor on paper
signed and dated '46 upper right
14 3/4 in. h. x 22 in. w

When abstract expressionism was coming into vogue, traditional artists like Clarence scrambled to adapt. Luckily, because he had a growing family to support, Clarence got a commission from Alcoa to paint local color in South America for their ads. These watercolors from that period were among my favorites as they express the layers of reality in indigenous cultures, the play between the physical and the spiritual that Clarence was aware of. Clarence was, in my opinion, the best watercolorist of his generation.

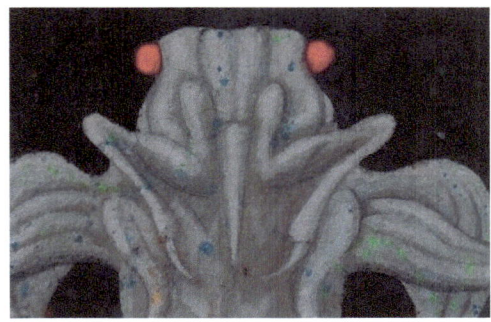

Cicada, 1960
watercolor scintilla
30 in. h. x 20 in. w.

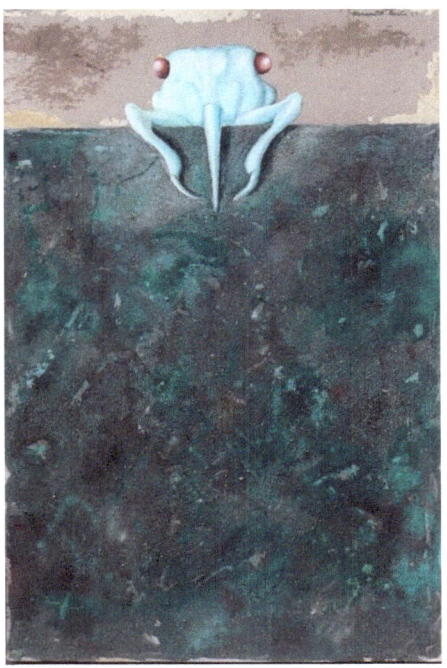

Over and Above Cicada, 1963
mixed media on cardboard
signed and dated upper right '63
30 1/2 in. h. x 20 in. w.

These were painted long before I came on the scene, but I always loved them because our wedding was in the year of the locust! Locusts fell from trees into champagne glasses and got stuck in hair sprayed dos.

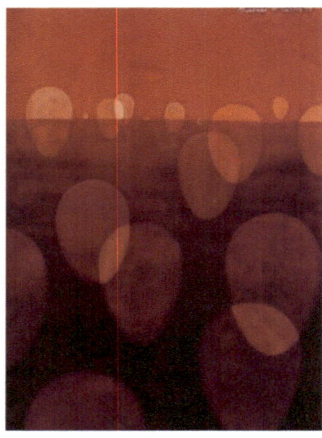

Eggs/Ovoids Over the Horizon, 1970
acrylic on paper
signed and dated '70 upper right
11 3/4 in. h. x 8 3/4 in. w.

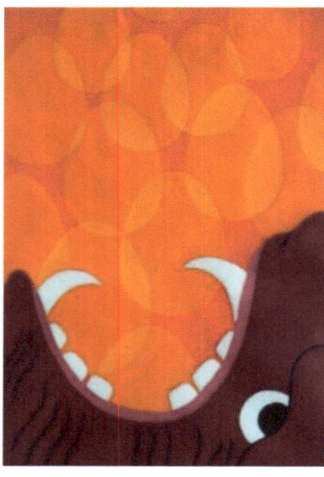

Chimera, 1972
acrylic on paper
signed and dated '72 lower right
10 in. h. x 6 3/4 in. w.

I'm partial to the work Clarence did in the early 1970s because it was when I entered the family. He was using the egg imagery then and his democratic use of them left me breathless. There are so many of us! And at heart, we are all just souls wandering—or maybe floating!—through the universe.

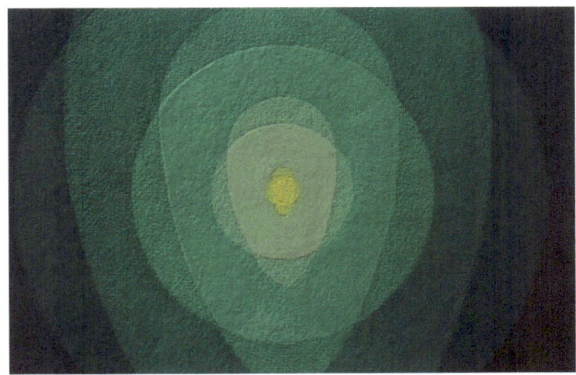

Green Mandala, 1970
acrylic on cardboard
signed and dated '70 lower right
15 in. h. x 11 in. w.

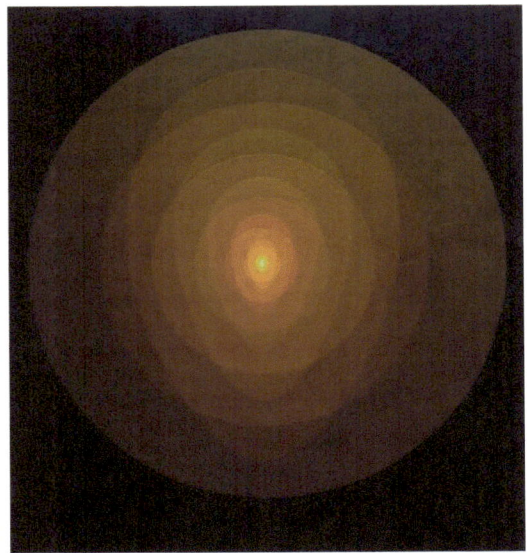

Icon #18, 1969
acrylic on cardboard
signed and dated '69 verso
21 1/2 in. h. x 32 in. w.

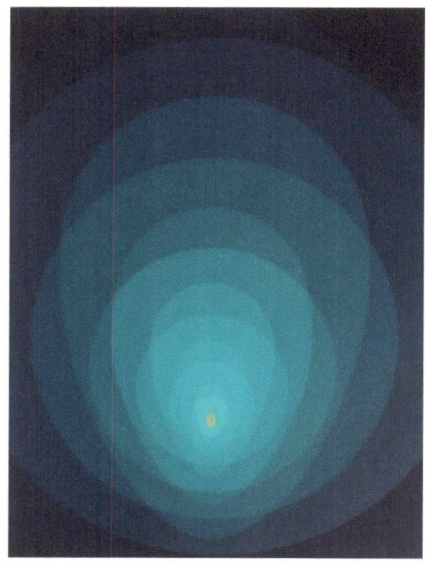

Blue Mandala, 1970
acrylic on scintilla
signed and dated '70 lower right
30 in. h. x 22 in. w.

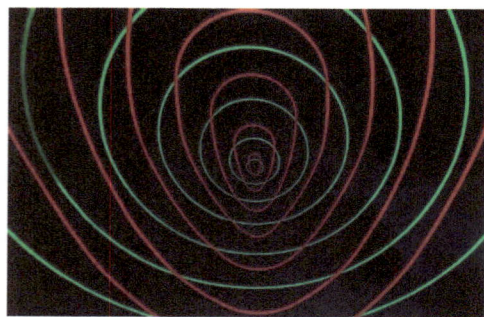

Green, Red and Black Mandala, 1969
acrylic on scintilla
signed and dated '69 lower right
24 3/4 in. h. x 18 in. w.

….the Mandalas! Nothing demonstrated Clarence's mastery of color more than the Mandalas which he painted segment by segment. I've seen them hung in old barns, in a millionaire's home on Lake Geneva, and in SoHo lofts. They are always the first thing to grab your attention and put you at peace with the universe. And yourself.

POOR MAN'S PULLMAN

I first met Clarence H. Carter on a train on the wall of the Philadelphia Museum of Art. The painting was called "Poor Man's Pullman" and was in the middle of a mélange of early to mid-century American art: Shawns, Singer-Sargents, Sloanes, Marshes, all hung above and besides each other as if in a sitting room whose wealthy owner had run out of space for meaningful arrangement of his acquisitions. The overall impression of the wall was crammed and muddy and I was drawn to Carter's vivid painting of two passengers on a train—a man looking directly out of the canvas at me and the back of a woman seated across from him wearing a cloche and staring out the window at the farmland chugging by. The seats were precise emerald green mohair and the patches of sun hitting the seats were a delirious lime. The cloche was a yellow that would fade in time, given enough sunlight. I remember thinking that the daisies in the basket on the seat by the gentleman would get sour a day after he gave them to whomever they were intended for, and did he know that about daisies? The scene in the painting was real, yet not painted with any aspiration for photographic representation. It was filled with light and magic, and I felt a kinship with the painter because he had articulated my still foggy vision of life: things fade and sour—the train may go off the track and down a precipice in the next moment—but they are illuminated and full of magic and, more than anything, they are precisely what they are.

I was at the Museum because I had recently placed in a political cartooning contest for students sponsored by the *Philadelphia Inquirer* and that small approbation, combined with my compulsive drawing and strong-arming of my bawling younger sister to sit still every day after school while I tried to get her eyes to line up right on canvas board with my brother's model airplane paint had given my father the idea that I was an artist. I certainly had demonic artistic drive. I drew over every blank surface including my homework, and my imagination was out of control. I made up stories about everything, which another family might have found precocious or even charming, but which alarmed mine who had had enough of dealing with magical grandmothers and aunts before the invention of Prozac. Everyone agreed that I should channel this mania, and since the clarinet and guitar they gave me weren't burning off my excess creative energy, they bought me my own paint. They gave me a Smith Corona portable electric typewriter for my twelfth birthday so I could write as fast as I was inventing things. When my best friend, Lydia, and I were kicked out of art class in our junior year for cutting up, we said to hell with them and after detention we painted madly on an entire tablet's worth of paper. Later, Lydia gave me her oeuvre and I gave her mine in what I thought was a show of defiance. Ten years ago, by happenstance, I ran into Lydia with her four year old daughter at a swimming pool and she introduced me as the "woman who painted the flamingo in our downstairs bathroom." She wasn't surprised when I told her then that I was painting portraits and working on short stories. "I thought you were going to explode," she told me as we reminisced about high school. "I thought we were having fun," I said, and was surprised that she had been a little afraid of me. "You were like a cyclone or something. All that energy."

So even though everyone else thought I was an artist, I didn't know what that meant. My family was black and blue collar Roman Catholic, and I had plenty of exposure to art before that Museum trip. Being in church every Sunday and holy day had made me chummy with art of the Italian Renaissance—at least in reproduction—and I had attended Catholic elementary school where we had "Picture Study" on Fridays. We read from pamphlet-size books with an old master picture on one side, always with a religious theme, and talk about the artist—Raphael, Millet, Michaelangelo—on the other side. I attended Catholic school for five years. At the rate of a painting a week, I was on a first name basis with probably a hundred and sixty masterpieces and knew the story behind each one. My mother's Byzantine Catholic church, which I attended when we visited her folks in the coal region, was filled with Russian icons and eastern imagery of saints and their bloody martyrdom. So, I had seen great paintings and had subliminally absorbed the lessons of color and composition. I thought art was about being holy and or dead, and my own urge to create had nothing to do with that. It also had nothing to do with the Picasso-esque—not in a good way—series of paintings I did of my sister finally wearing sun glasses to get rid of her pesky eye misalignment and sitting in front of a wildly skewed checkered tablecloth. What my urge to create did have something to do with was the atmosphere in that Carter on the wall of the Philadelphia Art Museum. I was increasingly curious about what kind of person could focus his energy to produce that kind of a painting. Because that was what impressed me the most about this little masterpiece: it was a controlled tempest. I spent months riding that train in my head.

At the time I wanted to be a journalist, and after one year at a local liberal arts college studying political science, I ran out of all the money I had earned since I was fourteen by shelving books at the library and subcontracting my brothers' newspaper routes. I pursued alternative enlightenment in Rasputin's Beef and Brew, a local hangout of the self-appointed intelligentsia whose owners forgot to card women. I met a man there, Blake Carter, who was supporting himself photographing and writing for a local rag while he wrote the great American novel and, did I want to see his photographs? Maybe read the great American novel? He was handsome, so, yes, I most certainly did.

Blake lived in the garret apartment of an old mansion in Fountain Hill, overlooking the steel mills in Bethlehem which were still brewing money and pollution. Almost every boy or man I met then had some connection with the steel company. Either they worked on the mill floor and pursued artistic or academic visions in their off time, or they were the scions of steel executives, lawyers, engineers who stuck around because they enjoyed the easy cachet of being atop the social hierarchy of a small city. The smog trapped us all—top dog and underdog—in the caste system of the feudal duchy of the steel mills. Blake was the first man I had met who had no real connection to the area, other than working at the newspaper, and that "only until I finish my novel" and I was gleeful at his dismissal of the citizens of our city as provincial. It thrilled me that he not only trumped social status by being an observer, but that he thought the whole structure was silly and irrelevant.

To put Blake's apartment in perspective: The homes of my father's peers were decorated with Hummel collections, intricate crosses woven from Palm Sunday fronds, military portraits of their men on top of the television, a cake on the table and coffee ready at a moment's notice to drink with that cake. The homes of my wealthier friends were decorated in an approximation of English country estates: dingy paintings featuring hunting dogs and horses wearing snotty expressions, heavily oiled furniture, leather bound books with uncut pages, sepia ancestors jailed in tarnished silver frames on the piano, walls painted dark teal, and everything marinated in single malt scotch. My own mother—ignoring the mandate of Bauhaus working class chic—fired decorator after decorator when she and my father built their new home, until she found one who helped her achieve her apparently long-simmering ecstatic vision of Versailles. I understood decorating as an embodiment of the heart's desire. So, when I walked into Blake's apartment it was like discovering a planet where people yearned for things I hadn't even heard of. At the top of the stairs was a reproduction of Fra Angelico's *Annunciation*. The walls of the long hallway were lined with fifteen other framed pieces, a couple of which were filled with reproductions of paintings I knew from Picture Study, the others weird images which were unknown to me but famous to the rest of the world—Hieronymous Bosch, Brueghel, Max Ernst—and photographs of beautiful women, as it turned out Blake also photographed models for their portfolios.

We smoked a little dope and he told me he had been a philosophy major in college because he got better grades in philosophy than history, his true love, and the scholarship/loan he got from the Mars Candy Company gave him money in proportion to his grades so he switched majors. We drank some red wine to toast the Mars Candy Company whose representative was very understanding, Blake said, when he called to collect and Blake told him he was broke at the moment, but would gladly pay them back when his novel became a best seller. His living room, which doubled as a study, had one wall covered floor to ceiling with a book case, a desk built into the middle of it, on the right side of which rested a stack of yellow paper on which he was typing his manuscript using a black enameled Adler, a romantic anachronism even then in the age of IBM Selectrics. A stack on the left held what was finished of his book. The sloping ceiling had just enough room for a stove pipe fireplace and a sofa which was a couple of foam cushions on top of an old door held up with cinder blocks, everything covered with a beautifully subtle piece—black and indigo—of Italian fabric. And which was incredibly uncomfortable. And so we went through the kitchen to get to the roof where we could look down on the steel mills while the wine and weed made us like each other more.

In the kitchen was a huge round unfinished oak table with claw feet, an unspeakably exotic touch, and on a bulletin board on the wall was a collage of headlines and photographs from the *National Enquirer*: "Boy Swallows Nickel but Five Pennies Come Out," "Five Year Old Girl Dying of Old Age" with a picture of a wizened face blowing out the five candles on a birthday cake, and "Man Nails Wife's Feet to the Floor so She Won't Leave." Blake told me that a football player friend who read the tabloids as if they were news had stayed with him one summer and, when the friend left, Blake made a collage out of them. "I find," he said, "this collage separates the wheat from the chaff. If you get it, you can be my friend." I had already decided I wanted to be his friend when a poster taped onto the side of the refrigerator caught my eye. A gray hairy spider was looking over a wall at me. It was a poster announcing an artist's show—long over—and the artist was Clarence H. Carter.

"That's so *funny*," I told him, "I saw a painting of his once. It was entirely different, but not really…"

"Yeah," Blake said, taking my hand and dragging me outside to the sulphurous air, not interested in talking about the poster or the artist. "He's my father."

I wasn't wised-up enough then to know that love isn't a mystery. Of all the hundreds of suitable mates there is always a reason you fall hard for that particular someone. I had been pressing my nose against the glass of a world filled with beauty, so when Blake casually opened the door for me, I stumbled in, falling in love with Blake at the same time I was falling in love with art and literature and music. Falling in love with life lived on a different plane of existence.

I didn't know if Blake and I would last the summer. This much I knew for sure, though: Whatever I had been before was over.

Clarence Carter and his wife Mary were in their third act when I met them for the first time, which was at the end of that summer when Blake and I picked them up at Newark airport from a trip to Europe. Major museums in the United States, including the Met and Moma, already owned Carters and he was represented by three galleries in New York City: Hirschl and Adler, Sid Deutsch, and Gimpel &Weizenhoffer. My arty peers in Bethlehem referred to him as an *eminence gris*. I was meeting a personage, not a boyfriend's father. In what I came to see what was typical Clarence he commandeered the wheel and so I really met the back of their heads. Mary, I learned later from Blake, thought I was a "little girl", which was true in both kind and unkind ways. Blake was a lot older and I was barely legal and I was just discovering the kinds of thing—Mozart, Thomas Mann, Max Beckmann—that comprised the main course of even their casual conversations. I realized too late during that ride home that the thing the nuns always said, "There's no such thing as a stupid question" was the worst piece of advice I ever received. Every time I opened my mouth, I dug myself deeper into the pit labeled "dumb Polack Catholic." I had been so sheltered I didn't even realize that some people hated Catholics. I might have redeemed myself if I had recognized the back of Mary's head from *Poor Man's Pullman* and said something clever or astutely observant about it. But naturally I didn't.

Right from the beginning the relationship between Clarence and me see-sawed from coldly polite to lukewarm to contentious. Clarence told Blake immediately after meeting me that I wouldn't be a social asset—an accurate assessment or not depending on what company you kept—and that I would be fat by the time I turned forty—which, okay, I put on a few pounds, but not *fat*. Clarence thought Blake needed a woman who would open social and economic doors for him, but Blake was not interested in marrying a girl like dear old Mom and he clearly didn't want those doors opened. If I had to classify Blake's and my relationship now, and granted it lasted a long time and went through numerous permutations, our early bond was based on both of us wanting to storm the gates of the magic kingdom of art, a kingdom that for Blake was embodied by his father. I came with Blake to its gates not knowing that the outcome of the assault had long ago been decided because the king who held the keys used them to unlock magic only for himself.

I might have formed a more forgiving opinion of Clarence if I had understood at the time that a large part of his ambivalence toward me was that I was an unwanted reminder of the ladder he'd had to climb up to leave where he'd come from. He'd been born into a working class family in Portsmouth, Ohio, a feeder city on a river below Pittsburgh and had attended The Cleveland Art School on money that his widowed mother confiscated from his sister's college tuition. He'd had to scramble to catch up with students from the big city schools. In an oral history in the Archives of American Art that Clarence recorded in 1964, he says, "I remember my first pathetic attempt at design. I was making little rosettes one right after the other making a repeat border which was rather sad." He came to the attention of William Milliken, the director of the Cleveland Museum, when he artlessly duplicated a Pieta by Antof Cardi. He'd received the museum's permission to copy the image, but nobody told him he wasn't allowed to simulate the Pieta's proportions and texture and a brouhaha over what some took to be an attempt at forgery ensued. The good thing that came of this was that Milliken became interested in Clarence and used his influence to sell a few of Clarence's paintings to collectors as well as the museum so he could go to study in Europe.

Money and class were always an issue with Clarence, and when I say that I fell for Blake with some hidden-even-from-myself-motives, Clarence had had a similar epiphany. In a scene right from the movie *Titanic*, Clarence met the love of his life, Mary Griswold, on the boat returning to America after a year studying in Italy. Because of his charm and good looks, he was able to jump from his third class berth to the parties in first class every night. When I met him, he still owned the matador suit complete with cummerbund he had bought in Spain and wore to those parties, which demanded either costume or white tie. It wasn't until the last night at sea that Mary Griswold emerged from her cabin where she had been suffering from sea-sickness and met the matador. Clarence was engaged at the time to a fiery fellow artist named Elizabeth Bart. Mary was a cool WASP goddess engaged to an attorney. She'd been courted by Norman Vincent Peale who—according to letters I found after both their deaths—was heartsick with losing her. By the time that night was over all previous entanglements were forgotten, barriers of money and class were breached, and Mary and Clarence were forever.

Their relationship was so tight there was little room for Blake and his older brother, John. Letters Mary wrote to her mother when she was pregnant contained a lot about her morning sickness and much about the dog, but little news of her sons after they were born.

Because I wasn't a door-opening socialite, Blake delighted in approval of me from people in his parents' circle. Vito Viviano, a sibling in a family whose matriarch, Catherine, was an art dealer in New York as well as neighbors with whom the Carters spent food holidays—Christmas Eve, Easter, Thanksgiving—proclaimed that I looked like I'd stepped off of a Renoir canvas when I walked into their country home with Blake for brunch one Easter morning wearing a large brimmed hat. Blake would trot that pronouncement out whenever Clarence challenged his choice of a soul mate. I was a Renoir! Although there was always the judgment that Renoir's women looked a little vulgar, and as we all knew Renoir started out painting dishes, even if they were Limoges. A dismissal of your worth could be accomplished only in the context of Western Civilization with footnotes. There were the great—and I quickly learned which artists, writers and composers to worship—and there was everyone else. And there was room for only one artist in the Carter orbit and that was Clarence. All others were relegated to the second team, and should be damn grateful to be allowed in the ballpark. In the Archives, Clarence says, "I think largely the person who is an intensively creative person…his main thought is himself…" Anyone say "Amen"?

After a stint as director of the fledging art department at Carnegie Tech (later Carnegie Mellon), Clarence moved his family to Hunterdon County, New Jersey buying an old farmhouse, outbuildings and acreage that had belonged to the Bohemian artist Wanda Gag, author and illustrator of *Millions of Cats*. It was a domain pulsing with creativity. Wanda's goal had been to have a sample of every living species planted there and she called her home All

Creation. By the time I came on the scene, the descendants of the millions of cats in Wanda's book still lived on Florian Young's farm across the road. When I took walks up the road at twilight, the cats would appear on the roof of his barn like a silent army mustering on a ridge for battle, until one started to cry and all joined in. A great horned owl who lived nearby kept them at bay. The raccoons, too, who screamed like witches at night by the creek, named *qui qua quomissicong* (the creek along which ducks waddle) by the Lenape who were there first. There was a line up the hill where a glacier had stopped millennia ago.

It was All Creation, fierce and gorgeous. Not one, but two great artists had chosen to live there. The first time I walked in the woods above the house, I knelt to touch the earth, feeling in the soil for the fingers of the creator.

The Carters held parties in the crumbling stone foundation of a barn that were attended by the type of people I had never met before: witty, sparkling, chic. The parties always ended up in Clarence's studio, guests offering tipsy suggestions and compliments on his work. Clarence listened non-commitally, never reacting.

Although Clarence once responded to a question by a local reporter about what he wanted for the new year, by saying "more trees, fewer people" the pictures I've seen of Gag's All Creation look like a mane of wild unkempt hair compared to the sculpted lawns Clarence favored. To showcase his paintings, the walls of the house were white, his studio's walls were dove gray, the wooden cabinets which housed his supplies were pale gray, even the rug which never had a splatter on it was off-white.

The humbling power of his art notwithstanding, All Clarence All the Time was maddening, stifling. No one except Billy Carter, Clarence's tabby cat, who disappeared sometimes for days, seemed to notice how hard it was catch your breath, to read your compass. I felt as if I were a character in Clarence's play, which may not have been an awful thing if I wasn't trying to write my own play. I tried to assert myself, insert some evidence of my independence. My first spring on

All Creation I planted twenty varieties of day lilies on a bank outside of a window of a new addition to the farmhouse. Clarence took me aside and told me that I'd broken up the clean line of the bank and let it go at that, but when I planted a row of zinnias outside his studio window he remonstrated full-family at breakfast that they were hybrids, read ugly. It was understood that I should dig them up. I didn't.

 Years later, barely able to speak because of a series of strokes, with hand waving grunts he made his displeasure known when I hung a string of tropical fish lights in the antique ten foot high hutch in the kitchen, because the kitchen needed some life. Or maybe it didn't. Irony is a tricky thing and I waded into it heedless of the discomfort my mischief might cause my mate who never in his life had thought to commit such daring acts of household deformation. Although my derring-do did free Blake up a little. Besides being a photographer and would-be novelist, Blake worshipped the great jazz saxophonists Getz, Webster, Sims, Hodges, Mulligan. He bought a saxophone at a pawnshop, and began to teach himself scales. Knowing better than to practice in Clarence's working orbit, he would walk far up into the woods and out of sight bleat for hours at a stretch.

 The part of All Creation that attracted me most was the upper studio, hidden from the eyes of the house and lower buildings. It was a cabin, a shack really, containing a day bed, a drafting table and a pot-bellied stove which figured in several of Wanda's woodcuts. Wanda purportedly sunbathed nude on the roof and took her lovers there. So, of course, it was the place I appropriated for myself when I was there.

 I was reading a book on the day bed one fall afternoon when a tall huntsman with a cross bow passed in front of the window, crunching through autumn leaves. When the hunter realized I was in the cabin, he knocked on the window and swung open the top half of the Dutch door to say hello. It was startling not only because the studio was isolated, but because the top half of a figure looking over a wall was exactly like Clarence's "Over and Above" series—animals peering over a flat wall—that he had painted in the sixties. When I asked Clarence if the Dutch door had inspired those paintings he smiled and said, "yes," as if I were on to him. But Clarence's yesses were always an if-you-want-to-think-so-why-not dismissal. He would tell you that the series started with a sympathetic encounter with his guard geese, Hector and Cora, who were mourning their unhatched egg. He said "yes" when someone asked him if Cora's dead egg, which he kept in his studio, was the inspiration for the ovoid shapes that dominated the last part of his career. I know now that he wasn't dodging an answer because inspiration doesn't come from only one source. It was the Dutch door AND the egg AND the sympathetic encounter with his geese AND the impossibly creamy color of their feathers AND the golden rectangle created by dividing a canvas into an open top and closed bottom.

When Blake and I were there, I drew on the drafting table in Wanda's studio with the same fervor as when I was in high school, still mostly cartoons. It was acknowledged in the Carter household that I had the makings of a superb cartoonist, an inferior talent to painting. Blake, who had plenty of his own visual talent, was relegated to only photography which we all knew wasn't a real art.

My cartoons had a weird perspective—buildings appeared to be running off the page—which everyone assumed was intentional. But it wasn't. I was frustrated by my inability to reproduce reality as my imagination plumbed it. When I told Clarence I wanted to paint, he hedged his encouragement, saying maybe I was an expressionist and while I pretended to agree, I knew that I wanted to capture the magic and light that I saw around me, not the distortion. I wanted the distortion to shape the hell up.

Blake and I lived in Europe for a lot of our life together, then Boston. On one pilgrimage to All Creation, we stopped in New York City and went to the Museum of Modern Art and, once again, I had the unsettling experience of going into a room, seeing a Carter on the wall and being as blown away as Saul on the road to Damascus. It was a painting of two women in cotton dresses and bonnets walking down a railroad track picking stuff off the ground and putting it in their baskets. Blake told me they were picking up coal that had dropped off a train, although French friends with us insisted that they were picking up *escargots*. For me, it illustrated the fact that anything you create takes on a life of its own and once he puts it out there the creator forfeits the right to its meaning. The scene depicted a dusk with a crescent moon seen only in dreams, and although you would swear you'd seen such a moon before, you would be unable to pinpoint just when and where. Great art's magic stops you in your tracks and reminds you of something you're certain you've always known but until that moment of recognition never articulated.

    One time at the farm, a canvas was rolled out on the floor of the living room. It was a luminous oil painting of an odd subject: Mary getting her teeth x-rayed at the dentist office. Clarence was debating whether to donate it to a man named Wolfson who was opening an art museum in Miami Beach. Clarence always refused these requests, saying that giving something for free demeaned the work of all artists, especially his, but it was a singular painting with no relation to any series and so not important. We left before he made a decision, and it was a forgettable event which I indeed forgot until a rainy day a few years ago when I was with my now-husband Paul in the Wolfsonian Museum in South Beach. Paul was, as usual, walking briskly ahead of me when he called from the next room, "You've got to see this painting!" Hello, Clarence.

    I decided to put some distance between myself and all the Carters by joining the army. A military doctor discovered that I had severe astigmatism which was what was making my world look like El Greco's. Glasses on nose I was stationed in Germany, and while taking classes at the University of Maryland in Heidelberg I found a painting teacher, Michael Kaspareck. He taught me photo realism, warned me not to become a painter's model because then I wouldn't be taken seriously, and advised me against having children unless I could afford full-time help. He told me he knew lots of women artists with babies on their hips and brushes in their hands and they were lousy mothers and lousy artists. Everything, Michael said, *everything*, he hammered, was secondary to your art.

Blake had told me a story about waiting for Clarence to pick him up for Easter break at a Friend's school, Oakwood, where he boarded for high school. All the teachers had left for spring break and he sat on the curb for four hours before Clarence finally roared up and yelled "Get in! I had a wash going." A painting in the works took precedence over being on time to pick up your kid.

Before Clarence fully succumbed to illness, I asked him if there was anything he regretted in his life and he said he was sorry about the effects of his temper on his family. But, he said, he wasn't sure he could have done it differently. He had things to do and no patience for domestic demands. Will and Ariel Durant, in <u>The Age of Reason Begins</u>, say "man has to pillage and destroy in order to create the space to create—do art." They were talking, of course, about the England of Shakespeare and the France of Descartes. They were talking about the studio in the New Jersey woods of Clarence Carter.

When Blake joined me in Germany I had a new stash of paintings to show him and this time the buildings were anchored on the earth and I didn't have to paint sunglasses over eyes to correct a misalignment. I was getting facile with glazes. Blake took slides of my paintings and the next time we went to the farm I was anxious for Clarence to pass judgment on them. I asked Blake, who had unlimited access to his studio, to show them to his father. Clarence, he reported back, held up the sheet of slides to the light, took one with a particularly challenging perspective out of the sleeve, and said, "She really botched that one. She shouldn't work from photographs. It flattens the perspective." And that was that. Clarence throughout the years had helped other artists get shows, lending his name to artists of lesser vision and skill, so at first I thought I was getting good in a way that was poaching on his turf. I'd tried for something difficult in that painting, but I see now that expecting him to applaud my daring was beginner's fantasy. It was my job as an artist to realize that vision and I hadn't. Clarence did me the favor of not showing me the kindness that, I have since learned in grad school and writing workshops, is doled out to those with no hope whatsoever. Mostly I found out that it's a mistake to show your work to people prematurely. Promise is not artistry. When you have created a world that seduces other people to enter, you don't need their affirmation. You can't keep them away.

After the army I got a scholarship to the School of the Museum of Fine Arts in Boston. Blake and I didn't have children so my idea of family was limited to Blake's and an occasional visit from my brother who lived in Norway, but being permanently back in the States meant being forced to confront my parents and siblings. By the time I'd reached 18 we'd grown tired of being incomprehensible to one other and Bathsheba in absentia was less of a strain on all of us. Living with a photographer, being part of a master painter's family, and being a painter myself, I'd begun to automatically think of everything as fodder for art. Art is removal from random consequences, and because I couldn't think of a visual way to express my feelings about my family I started writing short stories about them in which I was in control of the outcome.

I asked Clarence how he reconciled his family, nice earthy people, with the world he lived in as an artist. His painting had long ago stopped being about poor river culture and steel mills. Clarence said, "Families! It's just random who you're related to" and gave me a print of a large painting of his called, "Let Us Give Thanks" by way of explanation. In this painting Clarence, his mother Hettie, Mary, his sister Irene and her husband, son John and baby Blake, and a farm couple, cousins of his, are hunkered around a table, heads bowed in prayer before a turkey. I assumed this was some Thanksgiving gathering he remembered in oil. But it wasn't, Blake told me. What exactly was it then, this make-believe gathering? It was family as fodder.

Mary died in 1990. While she was failing was the first time in his life that Clarence stopped painting to tend to someone else. She had an old school bell that she rang when she needed something and Clarence made a big show of throwing the "damned bell" into the woods after her memorial service. We sprinkled her ashes around All Creation, me on those day lilies I'd planted years ago. Tabby Billy Carter didn't come home from his wanderings in the woods one day shortly afterwards. Clarence was alone.

Blake quit his job at the Bank of Boston and began splitting his time between Boston and All Creation. Clarence had always made a big deal of wanting to paint me, to force me I thought, remembering my German painting teacher's warning, from creator of my own world to actor in his. Perhaps sensing his demise he redoubled his demand that I model for him. I resisted by staying away. One weekend when Blake came home to see me, we got a phone call from a neighbor that Clarence had fallen and broken his hip.

I started commuting from Boston to New York by train every weekend. Blake would pick me up at Penn Station, we would have drinks in the Village then drive out to the country. For a non-drinker, I developed a giant thirst. I took to throwing elaborate house parties which Clarence, muted by a series of small strokes, couldn't protest. I became a Scotch expert and discovered Clarence's trick of hashing the booze: pouring cheap Scotch into Black Label bottles. Blake started working on a novel on the kitchen table and playing his saxophone in the attic.

On one train ride I met a Nigerian professor who was teaching at Brown. My brother was working in Nigeria at the time so I was interested in what he had to say. The beauty of trains is that if you have a sympathetic seat companion the time goes pleasantly and quickly Oko knew my entire life story. But Oko's real interest was his own. "You must write about what is happening to *us* in Nigeria." The oil business had ruined his country. The light given off by burning natural gas from the oil prevented animals from mating, so no hunting. The oil leaking into the delta destroyed the fish. It was a good story but Oko like everyone I was meeting wanted me to tell it from his point of view.

On another train ride I was sitting alone in a double seat when an older man wearing a pin stripe suit and running shoes put his bag overhead and sat next to me. He had old-world manners, bought me a coffee when he went to the club car. He was a Lebanese intellectual and wrote books about pre-Islamic literature. His latest literary venture was a novel and he asked me to blurb it. I told him a blurb from me would mean nothing because even though by this time I was writing more than painting no one knew who I was, but I gave him my Boston address and in a couple of weeks I received his manuscript which I read and endorsed. A few months later I received a little bound book with my blurb on the front cover next to a picture of an idealized Middle-Eastern beauty. I started receiving phone calls from Middle-Eastern men asking me for coffee.

Time spent on the train was like meditating and I had never before given myself this much time. I was finding it harder and harder to separate the physical world from the world in my imagination. Strangers on these train rides who bent my ear seemed as random as who I was related to and I would nod assent, lulling them with yesses I had no intention of honoring.

Clarence died in 2000. After his memorial service, we strewed his ashes around All Creation. I poured some on my zinnias and he'd be pleased to know that his old bones killed them. Blake and I started to unravel. I'd known for a long time that Blake's unfinished business with his father was more important to him than the emotional transaction he'd signed up for with me and we finally came undone after the exhaustion of remaindering Clarence's estate. As we were splitting up, Blake said: I was so intent on not marrying my mother I didn't notice I'd married my father.

Blake's nephew, Michael, his brother John's son who is head librarian at the Cloisters in New York, took charge of boxing up Clarence's archives and shipping them to the Southern Ohio Museum in Portsmouth, Ohio. Clarence is a favorite son, their second most famous after Roy Rogers. Clarence was a precise colorist and his studio contained files upon files of bits of color cut out of magazines, wrapping paper, ribbon. There were photos of his appearances at award ceremonies and graduations. There was a drawer full of lectures that he'd written in long hand on yellow paper and which I sat on his studio floor reading. They were amazingly engaging and smart. I was most interested, delighted actually, with the file drawers that contained the small format black and white photos on which, it turns out, he'd based most of his representational paintings, including the series of photos taken at different times and in different settings that he patched together to create "Let us Give Thanks."

I visited the Southern Ohio Museum this winter. I was there with Paul to deliver some charcoal nudes of Clarence's I'd found when I cleaned out Blake's and my Beacon Hill condo after Blake's death a few years ago. Works on paper are fragile and the fact that they were done in charcoal made me anxious to get them into professional care. Some of the paintings hanging in the Carter Wing I had already seen. Most I had seen only in reproduction. I was surprised, but shouldn't have been, at the museum's emphasis on his local origins and the pride of place for what they labeled his regional paintings. Clarence, even though he painted steel mills and coal heaps on fire early in his career, was not a regional painter and I understood now why that label galled him. It was just the imagery he'd used to house his magical vision. On the wall was a gorgeous portrait of his sister Irene. It wasn't the Aunt Irene with whom I shared a companionable fondness for vodka martinis and bridge, who found nature stifling and who proclaimed that being married twice was more than enough trouble for any woman. Irene may have been the model, but Clarence was the subject. The yellow jumpsuit she is wearing is infused with light, the material seeming to be spun by other-worldly creatures. She is sitting with one leg behind her, the other stretched out in front, poised for flight.

Like other representational artists in the 1950s, Clarence scrambled to find a new visual vocabulary when Abstract Expressionism became the only thing. He took advertising commissions from Alcoa and National City Bank in New York, which enabled him to pare down his figures and start experimenting with new form and color in his painting. The egg shapes that dominate his seductive geometric designs from the 1970s through the 1990s produced three series of work: Mandalas, Eschatos, and Transections. My own mother of the ecstatic Versailles vision once sat at a show for hours in front of these works. I found a letter in his archives from an American businessman in Japan, John Freeman, written to Clarence in 1990 about a Transection: "Sensie!" Mr. Freeman writes, "The cosmic dust that falls wherever you go has a powerful impact on those who are fortunate to be in your path of life."

I left the museum staff to their task of examining the charcoal nudes and slipped into Sara Johnson's office. Sara is the head curator of the museum and was a friend of Clarence's and Mary's. She had gone someplace warm for the winter and had graciously allowed me to use her office while I was there. She had left a note taped on her computer which said, among other things, "He was our delightful houseguest a couple of times, and even for all that personal time together, I think I knew only the public Clarence. I am eager to know as much as I can about Portsmouth's renowned native son and hope you will share your stories about the private Clarence."

The private Clarence? You can't take a walk in Portsmouth without seeing Kentucky across the river. On the drive from Pennsylvania you pass through West Virginia, by factories burning coal, by signs that say "Keep the EPA off our backs." The poverty of Appalachia is everywhere in Clarence's early paintings. Clarence wanted none of it. He used art to transport himself out of town. Shared stories? We both knew what it was like to be on the run from our beginnings, to find a more suitable vehicle for our imaginings. We didn't need to reminisce.

The private Clarence? The major reason people are fascinated with the private lives of artists is because--although I am an agnostic there is no other way to put it-- artists have seen the face of God. When I see flecks of yellow transposed over a field of blue in a Joan Mitchell painting I experience a breathless feeling of unexpected beauty that I think mystics must feel when they catch a spark of divine creation.

This is the private Clarence: on a wall mount at the Museum is Clarence's statement of the philosophy behind the "Over and Above" compositions:

The mysterious and magical elements in life have always captivated me, things suggested but only partly seen.

One element in this strange world of partial knowledge is the world of other creatures. We look at them in fascination and wonder. From this strange world of fact and fancy stare back images both real and unreal of what perhaps we might be to others, but never to ourselves—the Somebody Else.

The barrier creates a tension that heightens the mystery of the subject and isolates it from us. It is across this barrier that we perceive the silence and pervading mystery which transport the subject to the realm of conjecture.

I haven't abandoned painting, but for the past eight years, I have concentrated most of my efforts on writing fiction. I am startled when people ask if I am this or that character in something that I wrote. I am dumbfounded when editor, agent or reader demand that I personally have had to experience something to write about it. Because it's clear to me that whatever the sex or age or ethnic identity of any one of my characters they are a combination of me and random flecks of the reality I've lived through that got caught in my imagination. Do my words sometimes form themselves into something like art? It's possible. I hope so.

Sara Johnson told me to look through her files of letters and photos that Michael had hurriedly packed up after Clarence's death. It's unsettling to see them here, out of the context of All Creation. There is a funny picture of Clarence and Celeste Holmes at some black-tie shindig, Ms. Holmes looking radiant and camera ready, Clarence with his cheek full of hors d'oeurves, ignoring the mandate to never eat at those things because there are always photographers lurking. For a couple of hours I flip through photos of dignitaries giving Clarence awards, bittersweet photos of Clarence that Blake took, letters from Mary to her mother describing a world I'd been allowed to glimpse, until I start to feel a familiar sense of vertigo, of being out of step with a world I was barred from entering. Even if we drove ten hours to get here, and we'd planned to spend a couple of days, I want to flee.

Paul insists I walk through the gallery again. Who knows when we'll ever get back here? And Paul, clearly smitten by the world of Clarence Carter, leads me by the hand to confront Clarence one last time on the wall. His avatar gleams through Aunt Irene. Pigeons peer curiously at me over a Dutch door in an Over and Above. I smile, remembering that I watched Clarence paint that translucent egg that floats serenely through time in the midst of a Transection's intricate Italian architecture. Or did I? I hadn't arrived on the scene yet so I must have invented that memory. I'd like to think he'd appreciate that I'd found his long-lost charcoal nudes and delivered them to a place they would be seen and appreciated. Here's the truth: I don't know what he would think. Although I can imagine anything I like, and who will contradict me? Clarence's genius on the canvas touched a lot of people, including—emphatically—me. I appreciate that especially now, since his disappearing brand of magic makes him a rare bird. In Clarence's story, that makes him a hero. But when I tell the tale, he's just a guy I met on a train.

ABOUT THE AUTHOR

Bathsheba Monk is a novelist, playwright and screenwriter. She is the founder of Blue Heron Book Works, which specializes in memoirs and series fiction.
www.bathshebamonk.com
www.blueheronbookworks.com

www.ingramcontent.com/pod-product-compliance
Lightning Source LLC
Chambersburg PA
CBHW040333220526
45473CB00009B/2670